A Voice from J

Or, A Sketch of the Travels and Ministry of Elder Orson Hyde

Orson Hyde

Alpha Editions

This edition published in 2024

ISBN : 9789362992062

Design and Setting By
Alpha Editions
www.alphaedis.com
Email - info@alphaedis.com

As per information held with us this book is in Public Domain.
This book is a reproduction of an important historical work. Alpha Editions uses the best technology to reproduce historical work in the same manner it was first published to preserve its original nature. Any marks or number seen are left intentionally to preserve its true form.

Contents

INTRODUCTION. ....- 1 -
LETTER I. ....- 5 -
LETTER II. ....- 19 -
LETTER III.[A] ....- 24 -
LETTER IV. ....- 30 -
THE GATHERING OF ISRAEL. ....- 32 -

INTRODUCTION.

The circumstances which gave rise to this mission of Elder Hyde are quite peculiar and extraordinary; and in an American publication are thus described by himself: "Something near eight years ago, Joseph Smith, a prophet and servant of the Most High God, did predict upon my head, that I should yet go to the city of Jerusalem, and be a watchman unto the house of Israel, and perform a work there which would greatly facilitate the gathering together of that people: the particulars of which it is not necessary to mention here.

"Year after year has passed away since that period, and my labours in the ministry have been confined to the Gentiles on both sides of the Atlantic.

"In the early part of March last (1840), I retired to my bed one evening as usual, and while contemplating and enquiring out, in my own mind, the field of my ministerial labours for the then coming season, the vision of the Lord, like clouds of light, burst upon my view. The cities of London, Amsterdam, Constantinople, and Jerusalem all appeared in succession before me, and the Spirit said unto me, 'Here are many of the children of Abraham whom I will gather to the land that I gave to their fathers, and here also is the field of your labours.'

"A strict observance of the movements of the Jews, and a careful examination of their faith relative to their expected Messiah—the setting up of his kingdom among them, and the overthrow of the present kingdoms and governments of the Gentiles, will serve to open the eyes of many of the uncircumcised, when faithfully laid before them, that the great day of the Lord comes not upon them unawares as a thief.

"Take, therefore, proper credentials from my people, your brethren, and also from the governor of your state, with the seal of authority thereon, and go ye forth to the cities which have been shown unto you, and declare these words unto Judah, and say: 'Blow ye the trumpet in the land: cry, gather together; and say, assemble yourselves, and let us go into the defenced cities. Let the standard be reared towards Zion. Retire! stay not; for I will bring evil from the north and a great destruction. The lion is come up from his thicket, and the destroyer of the Gentiles is on his way, he is gone forth from his place to make thy land desolate, and thy cities shall be laid waste without inhabitant. Speak ye comfortably to Jerusalem, and cry unto her that her warfare is accomplished—that her iniquity is pardoned, for she hath received at the Lord's hand double for all her sins. Let your warning voice be heard among the Gentiles as you pass, and call ye upon them in my name for aid and for assistance. With you it mattereth not whether it be little or much; but to me it belongeth to shew favour unto them who show favour unto you.

Murmur not, therefore, neither be ye sorrowful that the people are slow to hear your petition; but do as has been told you. All things shall work together for your good if you are humble and keep my commandments; for it must needs be that all men be left without excuse, that a righteous retribution may be awarded to all.'

"Many other things were shown and told me in the vision which will be made public at the proper time and places. The vision continued open for a number of hours, that I did not close my eyes in sleep."

In obedience to the foregoing, Elder Hyde proceeded to lay the circumstances before the authorities of the church, and before the governor of the state of Illinois, who gave their hearty sanction to the mission, and from whom he obtained the following documents:

> *Letter of commendation from the Conference at Nauvoo, to Elders Orson Hyde and John E. Page, appointing and confirming their appointment to the work whereunto they have been called.*

> "To all people unto whom these presents shall come, GREETING.

> Be it known that we, the constituted authorities of the Church of Jesus Christ of Latter Day Saints, assembled in Conference, at Nauvoo, Hancock county, and State of Illinois, on this sixth day of April, in the year of our Lord, one thousand eight hundred and forty, consider an important event at hand—an event involving the interest and fate of the Gentile nations throughout the world. From the signs of the times, and from declarations contained in the oracles of God, we are forced to come to this conclusion. The Jewish nation have been scattered abroad among the Gentiles for a long period; and, in our estimation, the time of the commencement of their return to the "holy land" has already arrived.

> As this scattered and persecuted people are set among the Gentiles as a sign unto them of the second coming of the Messiah, and also, of the overthrow of the present kingdoms and governments of the earth by the potency of his Almighty arm, in scattering famine and pestilence like the frosts and snows of winter, and in sending the sword, with nation against nation to bathe it in each others blood; it his highly important, in our opinion, that the present views and movements of the Jewish people be sought after, and laid before the American people for their consideration,

their profit and their learning; feeling it to be our duty to employ the most efficient means in our power to save the children of men from the "abomination that maketh desolate," we have, by the counsel of the Holy Spirit, appointed Elders Orson Hyde and John E. Page, the bearers of these presents, faithful and worthy ministers of Jesus Christ, to be our agents and representatives in foreign lands, to visit the cities of London, Amsterdam, Constantinople and Jerusalem, and also other places which they may deem expedient; to converse with the priests, rulers, and elders of the Jews, and obtain from them all the information possible; and communicate the same to some principal papers for publication, that it may have a general circulation throughout the United States.

As Messrs. Hyde and Page have willingly and cheerfully accepted the appointment to become our servants and the servants of the public in distant and foreign countries for Christ's sake, we do confidently recommend them to all religious and christian people, and to ladies and gentlemen making no profession, as worthy members of society, possessing much zeal to promote the happiness of mankind; fully believing that they will be forward to render them all the pecuniary aid they need, to accomplish this laborious and hazardous mission, for the general good of the human family. Ministers of every denomination upon whom these gentlemen shall call, are requested to hold up their hands, and aid them by their influence, with an assurance that such as do this shall have the prayers and blessings of a "poor and an afflicted people," who have tested the depths of their sincerity, and love for their religion, by the sacrifice of their blood upon a land, shadowed by the stripes and stars of political and religious liberty.

Given under our hands at the time and place before mentioned."

(Signed) JOSEPH SMITH, JR., CHAIRMAN. ROBERT B. THOMPSON, Clerk.

From the Governor of Illinois.

QUINCY, ILLINOIS, April 30th, 1840.

Having been informed that the Revd's. Orson Hyde and John E. Page, elders in the church denominated Later Day Saints, are about to depart on their mission to Europe—and having heard the former gentleman preach—and having been made acquainted to some extent with the characters of both, it affords me pleasure to say, that I was much pleased with the sermon delivered by Mr. Hyde; and the reputation of both Gentlemen for talents and christian-like deportment, so far as I have been made acquainted, are unexceptionable; and as such, believe them to be entitled to the respect and kind treatment of all.

(Signed) THOMAS CARLIN, Governor of Illinois.

UNITED STATES OF NORTH AMERICA, State of Illinois, } ss:

I, Alexander P. Field, Secretary of State, of the State of Illinois, one of the United States of North America, and keeper of the great seal of said State, do hereby certify that Thomas Carlin, who took and signed the foregoing certificate, is now, and was at the time of signing the same, Governor of the State aforesaid, duly elected and qualified to office, with full power by the laws of this State to issue certificates as aforesaid; that said certificate is in due form of law, and that full faith and credit are due his official attestations.

In testimony whereof, I have hereunto set my hand, and the great seal of State, at the city of Springfield, this twenty-second day of May, in the year of our Lord, one thousand eight hundred and forty, and of the independence of the United States, the sixty-fourth.

(Signed.) A. P. FIELD, Secretary of State."

LETTER I.

Trieste, January 1, 1842.

DEAR BRETHREN OF THE TWELVE,

As the blushing orb of light from his eastern temple sends forth, this morning, over Alpine heights, his streaming columns of golden brightness to greet the earth with a happy new year, welcome its arrival, and crown it with a celestial radience, I might be justly charged with ingratitude towards a gracious and merciful Providence, and a want of generosity and reciprocal kindness towards my brethren, did I neglect to acknowledge the kind aid and protection which heaven has granted me in answer to your faith and prayers. Permit me, therefore, to commence my letter by wishing you all *"a happy new year;"* and through you, allow me to extend the same wish to all the saints, both in England and America; but *particularly to my wife and dear little children*.

I am happy to improve the opportunity, which this hour affords, of writing to you, and that happiness is increased by a firm conviction, that a letter from your unworthy brother, in the Lord, will be received by you with a friendship and cordiality corresponding to that which now animate my bosom.

Since it has pleased the Lord to grant unto me health and prosperity—to protect me from the dangers of the climates—from the plague and pestilence that have carried death and mourning on their wing, and return me again in safety to a land of civilised life, these things demand my highest gratitude, as well as demonstrations of praise and thanksgiving, to His exalted name.

As a member, therefore, of your honourable quorum, bearing, in common with you, the responsibility under which HEAVEN has laid us, to spread the word of life among the perishing nations of the earth, allow me to say, that, on the 21st of October last, "my natural eyes, for the first time, beheld" Jerusalem; and as I gazed upon it and its environs, the mountains and hills by which it is surrounded, and considered, that this is the stage upon which so many scenes of wonders have been acted, where prophets were stoned, and the Saviour of sinners slain, a storm of commingled emotions suddenly arose in my breast, the force of which was only spent in a profuse shower of tears

I entered the city at the west gate, and called on Mr. Whiting, one of the American missionaries at that place, to whom I had a letter of introduction from Monsieur Muratt, our consular agent at Jaffa. Mr. W. said, that in consequence of the unsettled state of his family, (having just removed to the house which he then occupied,) he was sorry to say it would not be convenient for him to invite me to share his hospitality; but very kindly went with me to the Latin Convent, which is a sort of hotel or home for strangers, and there engaged for me my board and lodging at a reasonable compensation, and said that he would keep a little watch to see that I was well taken care of. This expression of kindness did not escape my notice.

After I had been there an hour or two, Mr. Sherman, another American missionary, accompanied by a Mr. Gager, from America, who, I think, was a licentiate from the Presbyterian or Congregational Church, called on me, and after some considerable conversation upon the state of affairs in general, in America, I introduced to them the subject of my mission to that place; and observed, that I had undertaken to do a good work in the name of the Lord, and had come there for a righteous purpose, and wished their co-operation and friendly aid. They assured me that they should be happy to render me any assistance in their power to do good. I thanked them for their kindness, and observed, that as I had had little or no rest since I left Beyrout, I felt worn down with fatigue and a want of sleep, as well as being almost overcome by the excessive heat, and that I also wished to arrange some documents which I had, and then I should be happy to enjoy the privilege of an interview with them, and with Mr. Whiting at the same time. They said they would indulge me in my request at almost any time.

I had sent a lengthy communication to the Jews in Constantinople, in the French language, but had reserved a copy of it in the German. As this document set forth, clearly and plainly, the object of my mission there, I translated it into English in order that I might lay the facts before them in as clear a point of light as possible.

Accordingly, after wearied nature had sufficiently reposed under sleep's balmy and refreshing shade, I called on Mr. Whiting, according to previous arrangements, and Messrs. Sherman and Gager soon came in. After the usual salutations were passed, and all quietly seated, I expressed to them my gratitude for that opportunity of bearing testimony to the glorious reality, that the Lord was about to visit his people, and also my gratitude to HIM whose hand had been stretched out for my safety and protection, and also to bear me onward to the place where mercy, with all her celestial charms, was embodied in the person of his own Son.

I then took the liberty of reading the document containing the object of my mission there, and were it not for its length I would here insert it. After it was read, all sat in private meditation until Mr. Gager interrupted the silence by asking wherein the doctrines of our church differed from the doctrines of the established orthodox churches. I replied as follows: "There are so many different kinds of orthodox doctrines, all differing one from the other, that it might be difficult to determine which one to be the standard by which ours should be tried; but, said I, with your permission, I will set forth and explain to you the principles of our faith, and then you can determine for yourselves wherein they differ from others." So, beginning at the Ministration of the Angel of the Lord, I expounded unto them many things concerning the rise of the church, its organization and ordinances, and form and order of its government, after which Mr. Sherman spake as follows:

"Now, we are here trying to do all the good we can, and have been for some length of time; and what more would you have us do, or what more can we do?" I replied after the following: "It appears to me, even allowing your cause to be just and right, that your time is spent here to little or no purpose; not, however, that I would be understood as charging you with idleness or inattention; but the strong and deep-rooted prejudices which reign in the breasts of the people here against you, that they will not even allow you to educate their children, when you propose to do it gratuitously, must render your labours extremely limited; and, further, the genius of your policy does not admit of your making that exertion which the Saviour of the world required his servants to make in former days. You receive a salary from a home institution, and by that institution you are directed to remain here whether the people will hear you or not; whereas the Saviour taught his disciples to depart, and shake the dust from their feet, against that house, city, or people, that would not hear them, and not spend their labour for that which did not profit."

To this, Mr. Gager replied, "Although the fruits of our labours do not immediately appear, we ought not to be discouraged. We may labour, and other men may enter into our labours. The husbandman, after he hath sowed his seed, waiteth patiently until it hath received the former and latter rains; and, as the days of miracles are past, we cannot expect men to act now under the immediate direction of the Saviour as they then did." I might have here observed, that it would be a great tax upon the patience of the husbandman, if it did not quite exhaust it, to sow his seed year after year, and reap no fruits of his labour. But—

I replied, that miracles had truly ceased; but, said I, why have they ceased? Mr. Gager said, because they were not necessary. I made answer, that Jesus formerly said to the people, "according to thy faith be it done unto thee;" and said I, I presume he is of the same mind still; but the people have no faith in the power of God, therefore no miraculous favours are shown them; and because the religious would have lost sight of their high privileges, the horizon of their minds beclouded, and faith driven from their hearts by the vain and foolish traditions of uninspired men, the Lord hath sent an holy Angel from the Temple of Light, bearing to the earth truth's unfaded laurels, and has boldly asserted the rights and privileges of all who would seek the face and favour of the MOST HIGH. But against this heavenly message, streaming from the bosom of a compassionate God, with the purest love and good-will to a fallen race, and beaming in the face of men with a celestial radiance, is arranged the cold-hearted prejudices of an unbelieving world. Well did the Saviour ask this question, "When the son of man cometh, shall he find faith on the earth?" With this testimony have I come to Jerusalem; and in the name of my master, who here bore our sins, in his own body, on the tree, I warn all men, so far as I have opportunity, to beware how they lift their hands or their voices against it, for, by the voice of the Lord from Heaven, am I made a witness of the eternal reality of what I have declared.

Mr. Whiting then asked if we acknowledged any to be christians except those who embraced our doctrines and joined our church? To this I replied in the following manner: "We believe there are many in all the different churches, with many who are externally attached to no church, who serve the Lord according to the best light and knowledge they have, and this service is unquestionably acceptable in his sight; and those who have died in this condition have no doubt gone to receive the reward of their labours in the mansions of rest. But should He be pleased to send more light and truth into the world, or revive those principles of truth, which have been made to yield their sovereignty to the opinions of men, and they refuse to receive them, or walk in them, their service would cease to be acceptable to the Lord, and with no degree of propriety could we acknowledge them true christians; and we do know, and are sure, that the Lord has caused more light to shine, and that he will hold none guiltless who refuse to walk in it after the means of obtaining it are brought to their knowledge and placed within their reach." These were hard sayings. They observed, that they could not say that these things were not as I had said; but to them they appeared incredibly strange.

I then requested that some of them would do me the favour of an introduction to some of the principal Jews in the place: but this request was greeted with a number of *hems*, which commonly mean no more than to allay a little irritation, or tickling in the throat; but on this occasion, from the peculiarity of their tone and cadence, I judged they wished to be a little metaphorical, and so used the term figuratively to mean the following: "We have our scruples about complying with your request, lest it might detract from our influence and popularity." They observed that Mr. Johns, the English Consul, might be the most proper man to grant me the desired favour. I replied, that I knew as little of Mr. Johns as I did of any Jew in Jerusalem, but that I would not insist upon my request being granted. Mr. Whiting then remarked, that he should have no particular objections to do it, but that it could not be well attended to until a day or two hence. This reminded me of a circumstance in England, where duty once led me to call upon a clergyman to do me a little favour, but he said he could not grant it, because I had not come recommended by any one with whom he was acquainted. I replied, that I was very sorry to be so unfortunate on that occasion, as to be recommended by none but my master, who was the

Saviour of the world. The two are not exactly similar, yet the former reminded me of the latter. I thanked Mr. W., however, for his kindness, and our interview closed. The fact is, God has one system of etiquette, and reciprocity and this sign-seeking generation has another. The former is hospitality and kindness to the stranger; but the latter is—be very cautious and particular that you render him no assistance, neither show him favour unless he come recommended by our party, or by some others who are honourable and orthodox, like ourselves. But no man is justifiable in the eye of humanity, in the eye of the gospel, or in that eye that never sleeps, in rejecting the reasonable petition of a stranger, though he do not come clothed with letters from the chief priests, scribes, and elders of the people; and it is what no gentleman will do, unless his frankness and liberality have become blasted by the chilling winds of a sectarian atmosphere.

With what feelings of commingled pity and contempt does every Latter Day Saint, whose mind has thoroughly canvassed the principles of our faith, and in whose heart dwells that "unction from the Holy One," look upon that want of generosity and frankness, which he is often compelled to witness, when he knows that in his own bosom, independent of a boasting spirit, or any desire of vain glory, are jewels of light, truth, and knowledge, as far superior in lustre to any thing which they possess, as the purest diamond is to the common pebble of the rivulet!

I concluded, however, that I would try to discharge my duty before God, without subjecting any one to the humble mortification of giving me an introduction. For myself, I feel not very jealous of my popularity where the cause of truth requires me to hazard it, and am not so very particular. If my name be only recorded in heaven, on the list of the sanctified, it will abundantly compensate me for the sacrifice which duty calls me to make of it among men. Let them, therefore, look upon me as they may, a deceiver or a deceived, a wise man or a fool, I feel very thankful to the Lord for what mine eyes have seen, mine ears have heard, and, more than all, for what my soul has experienced; and it is my constant prayer to an over-ruling Providence, that his free grace may be amply sufficient to bear me triumphantly through life's conflicting scenes, that my poor heart may swell the notes of praise and thanksgiving for ever and ever to HIM who died to save me and wash me from my sins, in his own most precious blood.

Summoning up, therefore, what little address I had, I procured a valet d'place, or lackey, and proceeded to the house of Mr. Simons, a very respectable Jew, who, with some of his family, had lately been converted and joined the English Church. I entered their dwelling. They had just sat down to enjoy a dish of coffee; but immediately arose from the table to meet me. I spake to them in German, and asked them if they spoke English; they immediately replied "Yes," which was a very agreeable sound to my ear. They asked me, in German, if I spoke English. I replied, "Ya, Mein Herr." I then introduced myself to them, and, with a little apology, it passed off as well as though I had been introduced by the Pacha. With that glow of warmth and familiarity, which is a peculiar trait in the German character, they would have me sit down and take a dish with them; and as I began to relate some things relative to my mission, the smiles of joy which sat upon their countenances, bespoke hearts not altogether indifferent. There are two ministers of the Church of England there. One was confined to his bed by sickness, and the other, a German, and a Jew by birth, soon came in. After an introduction, I took the liberty to lay open to him some of our principles, and gave him a copy of the communication to the Jews in Constantinople to read. After he had read it, he said that my motives were undoubtedly very good, but questioned the propriety of my undertaking, from the fact that I claimed God had sent me. If, indeed, I had gone to Jerusalem under the direction of some missionary board, or society, and left God out of the question altogether, I should have been received as a celestial messenger. How truly did our Saviour speak, when he said, "I am come in my father's name, and ye receive me not; but if another were to come in his own name, him ye would receive." I replied, however, that so far as I could know my own heart, my motives were most certainly good; yet, said I, no better than the cause which has brought me here. But he, like all others who worship a God "without body or parts," said that miracles, visions, and prophecy had ceased.

The course which the popular clergy pursue at this time in relation to the Divine economy, looks to me as though they would say; "O Lord! we will worship thee with all our hearts, serve thee with all our souls and be very pious and holy. We will even gather Israel, convert the heathen, and bring in the millennium, if you will only let us alone that we may do it in our own way, and according to our own will. But if you speak from heaven to interfere with our plans, or cause any to see visions or dream dreams or prophecy whereby we are disturbed or interrupted in our worship, we will exert all our strength and skill to deny what you say, and charge it home upon the devil or some wild fantastic spirit, as being its author."

That which was looked upon by the ancient saints, at among the greatest favours and blessings, viz., Revelation from God and communion with him by dreams and by visions, is now looked upon by the religious world as the height of presumption and folly. The ancient saints considered their condition most deplorable when Jehovah would not speak to them; but the most orthodox religionists of this age deem it quite heterodox to even admit the probability that he ever will speak again. O, my soul! language fails to paint the absurdity and abomination of such heaven-opposing, and truth-excluding dogmas; and were it possible for those bright seraphs that surround the throne above, and bask in the sunbeams of immortality, to weep over the inconsistency and irrationality of mortals, the earth must be bedewed with celestial tears. My humble advice to all such is, that they repent and cast far from them these wicked traditions, and be baptized into the new and everlasting covenant, lest the Lord speak to them in his wrath, and vex them in his sore displeasure.

After some considerable conversation upon the priesthood and the renewal of the covenant, I called upon him to repent and be baptized for the remission of his sins, that he might receive the gift of the Holy Ghost. What! said he, *I* be baptized! Yes, said I, *you* be baptized. Why, said he, I have been baptized already! I replied something after the following: "You have, probably, been sprinkled, but that has no more to do with baptism than any other ordinance of man's device; and even if you had been immersed, you would not have bettered your condition, for your priesthood is without power. If, indeed, the catholic church had power to give you an ordination, and by that ordination confer the priesthood upon you, they certainly had power to nullify that act, and take the priesthood from you; and this power they exercised when you dissented from their communion, by excluding you from their church. But if the catholic church possessed not the priesthood, of course your claims to it are as groundless as the airy phantoms of heathen mythology: so view the question on which side you may, there is no possible chance of admitting the validity of your claims to it. Be it known, therefore, that ordinances performed under the administration of such a priesthood, though they may even be correct in form, will be found destitute of the seal of that authority by which heaven will recognise his own in the day when every man's work shall be tried: though a priesthood may be clothed with the wealth and honours of a great and powerful nation, and command the respect and veneration of multitudes whose eyes are blinded by the thick veil of popular opinion, and whose powers of reflection and deep thought are confused and lost in the general cry of "great is Diana of the Ephesians," yet all this does not impart to it the divine sanction, or animate it with the spirit of life and power from the bosom of the living God; and there is a period in future time, when, in the smoking ruins of Babel's pride and glory, it must fall and retire to the shades of forgetfulness, to the grief and mortification of its unfortunate votaries.

In consequence of his great volubility, I was under the disagreeable necessity of tuning my voice to a pretty high key, and of spacing short between words; determining that neither his greatness nor learning should shield him from the shafts of a faithful testimony: but there is more hope of those Jews receiving the fullness of the gospel, whose minds have never been poisoned by the bane of modern sectarianism, which closes the mouth of deity, and shuts up in heaven all the angels, visions, and prophecyings.

Mrs. Whiting told me that there had been four Jewish people in Jerusalem converted and baptized by the English minister, and four only; and that a part of the ground for an English church had been purchased there.

It was by political power and influence that the Jewish nation was broken down, and her subjects dispersed abroad; and I will here hazard the opinion, that by political power and influence, they will be gathered and built up; and, further, that England is destined, in the wisdom and economy of heaven, to stretch forth the arm of political power, and advance in the front ranks of this glorious enterprise. The Lord once raised up a Cyrus to restore the Jews, but that was not evidence that he owned the religion of the Persians. This opinion I submit, however, to your superior wisdom to correct, if you shall find it wrong.

There is an increasing anxiety in Europe for the restoration of that people; and this anxiety is not confined to the pale of any religious community, but it has found its way to the courts of kings. Special ambassadors have been sent, and consuls and consular-agents have been appointed. The rigorous policy which has hitherto characterised the course of other nations towards them, now begins to be softened by the oil of friendship, and modified by the balm of humanity. The sufferings and privations under which they have groaned for so many centuries, have at length touched the mainsprings of Gentile power and sympathy; and may the God of their fathers, Abraham, Isaac, and Jacob, fan the flame by celestial breezes, until Israel's banner, sanctified by a Saviour's blood, shall float on the walls of Old Jerusalem, and the mountains and valleys of Judea reverberate with their songs of praise and thanksgiving to the Lamb that was slain!

The imperial consul of Austria, at Galatz, near the mouth of the Danube, to whom I had a letter of introduction from his cousin in Vienna, told me, that, in consequence of so many of their Jewish subjects being inclined of late to remove to Syria and Palestine, his government had established a general consulate at Beyrout for their protection. There are many Jews who care nothing about Jerusalem, and have no regard for God. Their money is all the god they worship; yet there are many of the most pious and devout among them, who look towards Jerusalem as the tender and affectionate mother looks upon the home where she left her lovely little babe.

You will discover by this letter, and more particularly by the one written from Alexandria, to Elder Pratt in Manchester, England, that, through the goodness of the Lord, I have been enabled to accomplish that which was told me prophetically, several years ago, by Brother Joseph Smith.

Though the blustering snow-storm has thrown the gorgeous folds of his crimson mantle over the mountain tops, which half encircle us on our north and east as we lie here in quarantine, yet their sides towards the base, beautifully terraced and thickly set with vines and olives, though not in their summer dress, present a widely-extended scene of rural beauty and loveliness. All the irregularities and deformities of nature (if, indeed, there are any,) are completely lost in the distant view, though we gaze through the ship's powerful magnifier; so, when the eye of imagination surveys the saints far in the west, their faults and foibles are lost in the distance, (if, indeed, any they have,) and nothing but their virtues appear, which render the society very inviting and extremely desirable. The simple unrestrained language of my heart is—I want to see my brethren, for in their bosoms, I am sure, is a corresponding echo which,—

> Like the harp, when the zephyr is sighing
> To the breath of that zephyr, in music replying,
> Friendship can tremble with feelings as true.

I have just been upon deck to witness the king of day retiring in his robes of state to the western portions of his kingdoms, to proclaim there, in *propria persona*, the advent of 1842, after opening and lighting up the glory of the new year in the east. As his golden disk was sinking behind the western rim of the deep blue waters of the Adriatic, and throwing back, in rich profusion, his soft and glowing beam upon the clear blue sky, with a radiance and splendour peculiar to none but him, thought I, oh, that thou couldest take a thought or good wish from me and bear it on the pathway of one of thy golden beams to my dear little family, which perhaps at this moment is pouring his noon-day splendour obliquely upon the home where they dwell. But another thought succeeded—I will not be a Parsee. There is a Being whose throne is high, and whose glorious image shines forth in the mirror of all his works to feast the mental eye and heal the wounded heart, "His ear is not heavy that he cannot hear, neither is his arm shortened that he cannot save;" to HIM, therefore, will I send a thought on the wing of my evening devotion, and breathe an aspiration that his favour may gladden and cheer the cot where dwell all my earthly hopes and earthly riches: therefore, tarry not for me thou glorious orb of light, but speed thy course onward in the circuit of the heavens, to dye the sheen of other climes, and to roll in the hour when the dead, small and great, shall stand before God.

Jerusalem at this time contains about twenty thousand inhabitants; about seven thousand are Jews, and the remainder mostly Turks and Arabs. It is enclosed by a strong wall from five to ten feet thick. On those sides which are most accessible, and consequently most exposed to an attack, the wall is thickest, and well mounted with cannon; it is from twelve to thirty feet in height. The city is situated at the south-eastern extremity of an inclined plane, with the valley of Kedron on the east, and the valleys of Hinnom and Gihon on the south and west, all converging to a point in the valley of Jehosaphat, south-east of the city: from the eastern gate of the city to the top of Mount

Olivet, as you pass through the valley of Kedron, is just about one English mile. On the top of this mount you have a fair view of the Dead Sea and river Jordan, which are about fifteen miles in the distance. As I stood upon this almost sacred spot and gazed upon the surrounding scenery, and contemplated the history of the past in connection with the prophetic future, I was lost in wonder and admiration, and felt almost ready to ask myself—Is it a reality that I am here gazing upon this scene of wonders? or, am I carried away in the fanciful reveries of a night vision? Is that city which I now look down upon really Jerusalem, whose sins and iniquities swelled the Saviour's heart with grief, and drew so many tears from his pitying eye? Is that small enclosure in the valley of Kedron, where the boughs of those lonely olives are waving their green foliage so gracefully in the soft and gentle breeze, really the garden of Gethsemane, where powers infernal poured the flood of hell's dark gloom around the princely head of the immortal Redeemer? Oh, yes! The fact that I entered the garden and plucked a branch from an olive, and now have that branch to look upon, demonstrates that all was real. There, there is the place where the Son of the Virgin bore our sins and carried our sorrows—there the angels gazed and shuddered at the sight, waiting for the order to fly to his rescue; but no such order was given. The decree had passed in heaven, and could not be revoked, that he must suffer, that he must bleed, and that he must die. What bosom so cold, what feelings so languid, or what heart so unmoved that can withhold the humble tribute of a tear over this forlorn condition of the Man of Sorrows?

From this place I went to the tombs of the prophets in the valley of Jehosaphat, and on my way around the city, I entered the pool of Siloam and freely washed in its soft and healing fountain. I found plenty of water there for baptizing, besides a surplus quantity sent off in a limpid stream as a grateful tribute to the thirsty plants of the gardens in the valley. The pool of Bethsda, which had five porches, yet remains in the city, but in a dilapidated state, there being plenty of water to meet the demands of the city of a better quality, and more convenient—this vast reservoir is consequently neglected. This pool was unquestionably as free and accessible to all the people of Jerusalem as the Thames is to the Cockneys, or the Mississippi to the people of Nauvoo; and from its vast dimensions, it would certainly contain water enough to immerse all Jerusalem in in a day: so the argument against the doctrine of immersion, on the ground that there was not water enough in Jerusalem to immerse three thousand persons in in one day, is founded in an over anxiety to establish the traditions of men to the subversion of a gospel ordinance; and it will be borne in mind also, that the day of Penticost was in the month of May, just at the close of the rainy season, when all the pools and fountains in and about the city were flush with water.

What were anciently called Mount Zion and Mount Calvary, are both within the present walls of the city. We should not call them mountains in America, or hardly hills; but gentle elevations or rises of land. The area of what was called Mount Zion, I should not think contained more than one acre of ground; at least as I stood upon it and contemplated what the prophets had said of Zion in the last days, and what should be done in her, I could no more bring my mind to believe that the magnet of truth in them which guided their words, pointed to this place, any more than I could believe that a camel can go through the eye of a needle, or a rich man enter into the kingdom of God. But on the land of Joseph, far in the west, where the spread eagle of America floats in the breeze and shadows the land—where those broad rivers and streams roll the waters of the western world to the fathomless abyss of the ocean—where those wide-spreading prairies (fields of the wood) and extensive forests adorn the land with such an agreeable variety, shall Zion rear her stately temples and stretch forth the curtains of her habitation. The record of Mormon chimes in so beautifully with the scriptures to establish this position, that an honest and faithful examination of the subject is all that is required to expel every doubt from the heart.

The customs and manners of the people of the east are so similar to what they were in the days of our Saviour, that almost everything which the traveller beholds is a standing illustration of some portion of scripture: for example, I saw two women grinding wheat at a little hand-mill, consisting of two small stones with a little rude tackling about it, the whole of which one man might take in his arms and carry almost any where at pleasure. One would turn the top stone until her strength was exhausted, and then the other would take her place, and so alternately keep the little grinder in operation. It appears that our Lord foresaw the perpetuity of this custom, even to the time of his second coming; for he said, "Two women shall be grinding at the mill; one shall be taken and the other left; and for aught I know, these two I saw were the identical ones. I also saw the people take a kind of coarse grass and mix it with some kind of earth or peat that had been wet and reduced to the consistency of common mortar, and then lay it out in flattened cakes to dry for fuel. I then, for the first time in my life, saw the propriety of our Saviour's allusion, "If God so clothe the grass of the field, which to-day is, and tomorrow is cast into the oven, &c." I might swell this letter to a volume upon these subjects, but I forbear for the present. One may read of the customs of the East, but it is not like seeing them. To read of a good dinner may brighten up a man's ideas about eating, especially if he be a little hungry; but to sit down at the luxurious board and eat is far more satisfactory. The two cases are not exactly parallel, yet the latter serves to illustrate the former.

As I walked about the environs of the town, my spirit struggled within me in earnest prayer to the God of Abraham, Isaac, and Jacob, that he would not only revolutionize this country, but renovate and make it glorious. My heart would lavish its blessings upon it in the greatest prodigality in view of what is to come hereafter. After returning to the city, I found my feet and legs completely coated with dust; for the whole face of the country was like an ash bed in consequence of the great length of the dry season. I then thought how very convenient it must have been for the ancient disciples to fulfil one injunction of the Saviour, "shake off the dust of your feet."

Syria at present is in a very unsettled state. The Drewzes and Catholics are fighting almost constantly. They sometimes kill hundreds and hundreds of a day. In some sections it is not unfrequent that the traveller meets some dozen or twenty men by the way-side without heads, in a day. In a letter from Bavaria, I stated that hostilities had recommenced between the Turks and Egyptians; I took the statement from a German paper, but it was a mistake. The hostilities were between the lesser tribes in Syria. The American missionaries at Beyrout and Mount Lebanon have received official notice through Commodore Porter, our minister at Constantinople, from the Grand Sultan, that hereafter they can have no redress by law for any violence, outrage, or cruelty, that may be practiced upon them by the people; and advises them to leave the country. This course is approved of by Commodore Porter. I read the correspondence between him and Mr. Chassan, our consul at Beyrout; but all is going on in the providence of God. Syria and Palestine must ferment and ferment, work and work, until they work into the hands of Abraham's children to whom they rightly belong; and may the God of their fathers bless the hand that aids their cause.

I must now begin to think of coming to a close. I have nearly three weeks yet to remain in quarantine. The time seems long; yet I endeavour not to let it run to waste. When our ship shall have obtained her prattique, I shall proceed, if the Lord will, directly to Germany over the Alps, and try to light up a fire there. Will you give me your prayers that God may bless my exertions, and that I may be enabled to conduct myself with that dignity and propriety in all things which become a man of God, and which the purity and virtue of the cause I advocate, so justly merits; and further, that in my great weakness celestial strength may appear.

My kind respects to the presidency of the church, and a happy new year to all absent and enquiring friends.

With the most kind and tender feelings towards you, and with a heart that will burst with blessings on your heads when your faces I behold, allow your *unworthy* brother in Christ to close by the following lines which he offers you as a farewell token until Providence shall permit us again to meet:

> Where the sun leaves his last golden ray,
>   Far over the sea's swelling tide,

Will friends, dear and true, for me pray,
  That I in the Lord may abide?
Though distance and time do us part,
  And scenes new and strange roll between,
Your memory is dear to my heart,
  And friendship's bright star gleams the same.

In the west, let its ray pour a light
  On the circle of Zion's true sons,
To greet them with joy in the sight
  Of Him who has said we are one.
To share in the spoils of my love,
  Her daughters, though last, are not least;
For surely, 'twas blest from above
  Which graced the end of the feast.

ORSON HYDE.

DEAR BROTHER PRATT,

In consequence of the great distance to Nauvoo, and the uncertainty of this letter reaching our brethren there, should I address it to them, I have thought proper to address it to you, with this request, that you will publish it by itself in pamphlet form, as soon as possible, and send a copy to each one of the twelve, three to the presidency of the church, and one to my wife. I wrote her a lengthy letter from this place, and sent it by an American ship bound directly to New York, and should have sent this along with it if it had been ready. I wish you, also, to send five copies to my brother, Abijah Hyde, Oxford, Newhaven County, and State of Connecticut, that he may send one to each of my other brothers, and one also to each of my sisters, and that I wish them and their families to consider themselves embraced within the circle of every good wish expressed in it.

The size of the edition I leave with you to determine. You know that I, like yourself and every other Latter Day Saint preacher, have no salary except the voluntary contributions of the people where we labour; and having been absent from my family nearly two years, my arm and my purse have been too short to render them much assistance. I wish you, therefore, to forward a sufficient number of copies to each branch of the church any where this side of the Atlantic, that all who wish for a copy may have one; and whatever any brother, sister, or friend, shall be disposed to give in return, for the benefit of my wife and children, will be most gratefully received by them, and no less so by me. It can be handed to the agent to whom you shall send the copies, and he can forward it to you through the post, or otherwise as you shall direct, which will enable you to pay the printer; and the balance (should there be any) I will advise you in due time how to convey it to my family. But should you discover any impropriety in the plan, or should it be inconsistent for you to carry it into execution, you are at liberty to use the document as your better wisdom may direct you, only send it in some form to Nauvoo as soon as possible. Perhaps I feel too anxious about my family, but where the heart has only few objects to share its sympathies, upon those few objects the sun of affection shines with warmer and more brilliant ray. My family is my earthly all; and of late my feelings concerning them are very peculiar. It is nearly a year since I have heard anything of them, and being confined here in quarantine, perhaps I have become childish. My kind respects to yourself and family, to brothers Snow and Adams, and to all the Saints in England; may God bless you all: pray for me. I am your brother in Christ,

ORSON HYDE.

P.S. In justice to the American missionaries at Jerusalem, I must say, however, particularly of Mr. Whiting, with whom I became most acquainted, that as men, their conduct towards me was both courteous and civil; and when I left Mr. W.'s house I could not withhold my blessing from himself and family—his interesting wife and lovely little girls, who all speak fluently the English and Arabic. A kind word or action towards a stranger in a strange land is not soon forgotten. May the Lord bless them and their families with his salvation, through the knowledge of the truth, was my desire then, and is my prayer still.

Note.—Expecting a letter or letters from you to be lodged in Bavaria for me, I have addressed a note there requesting them (if any) to be forwarded to me at this place; but as my note went on shore in the bustle without the postage being paid, and having to pass through different kingdoms, I do not expect it will be forwarded. I hope, however, to get news from you and the church when I get there myself. I hope also to hear something from my wife. I feel that a word from her would be more precious than gold; yet I am afraid to hear lest she may be in trouble, or some of her friends dead—a father or mother perhaps, or brother or sister. Yet I try to comfort myself with the thought that my long absence is the cause of all my bad feelings. The Lord knows, and I pray that he may bind up every broken heart. Fare-thee-well; thy brother in the Lord,

O. H.

LETTER II.

Trieste, January 17, 1842.

DEAR BRETHREN AND SISTERS AT NAUVOO,

I have just written a lengthy letter to the Twelve, and sent it by way of Elder Pratt, in England. In that, and in a former one written to him from Alexandria in Egypt, is contained an account of my mission to Jerusalem. I feel, however, as though I wished to write a few lines more on this the last day of my confinement on ship board, where I have spent the last fifty-six days: six days in the harbour of Alexandria—twenty-two days on our passage—and twenty-eight here in quarantine. To-morrow, if the Lord will, the the jubilant song, with its thrice welcome melody, will greet the ears of a poor captive exile, the prison doors give way, and he be permitted once more to breathe the air of freedom in a land where he is not annoyed by the sight of the star and crescent, the turban and the covered face—all of which are an abomination in my sight.

The thoughts which I record will, no doubt, be scattering, and like "the gleaning of grapes when the vintage is done;" or like a few indolent belated stragglers going to the place of worship on a Sabbath morning after the more conscientious and faithful have broken the silence which hovered around the place of their devotion, and greeted the morning with their prayers and joyful acclamations of praise to the Lord their God.

It is now rapidly advancing to the close of two *long* years since I had the pleasure of mingling my voice with yours in ascribing honour and thanksgiving to that Being whose arm alone has been my support, and whose kind angel has swept the misty vapours far away which dispondency would feign cast over the star of hope, and nearly one year since I have heard ought direct from you. While in Bavaria, I saw a statement in a German paper that Brother Joseph had been apprehended and confined in prison. I knew not but that it might be so; yet I was inclined to set it down among the numerous deaths which he has suffered, the imprisonments which he has endured, and the various runaways of which he has been guilty, according to the flood of newspaper slang which has been poured forth upon a deceived public: but as time allows nothing to remain stationary, you may judge of my anxiety to hear from you, particularly when the happiness or misery of my own dear wife and little children is identified with your own.

I sometimes fancy myself in your midst, in my hours of silent meditation, gazing upon a large concourse of saints. I see many, *very* many strange faces that I never saw before; while others with whom I was familiarly acquainted, I do not see. Being anxious to know where they are, I inquire after them; but am told, with a sigh that contains no fiction, that time—that cruel and unfeeling destroyer of the human race, has borne them on his untiring wing to a long and sleepy mansion, to await the hour when the voice of the Archangel and the trumpet of God shall bid their sleeping dust arise, and come forth to receive the reward of their labours. O, ye precious souls! your debt is paid, and I cannot but embalm your memory with a tear as these lines slip from my pen.

There, for instance, sits a brother looking steadily upon his little daughter. His melancholy mien bespeaks a heart wadeing deep in sorrow: he puts his handkerchief to his face and bursts into tears. I ask the cause of that; and am told, that that brother has lately lost his wife; and as he looked upon the young and tender flower, and recognised in her the kind and affectionate features of the companion of his youth who now sleeps in the arms of death, he immediately contrasted all her virtues with every unkind word that he might have given her, and every ungenerous action; and the thought that his children are bereft of a mother, and his own bosom of its dearest friend, swells his heart to a burst of grief; and every unkind word which he might have given her in the warmth of the moment, now rushes upon his memory, pierces his soul, and adds an additional pang to the flood of grief which overwhelms him. "Husbands," whoever you are, "love your wives, and be not bitter against them." The delicacy of their sex, the vivid perceptibility of their mind, and the soft and engaging virtues of their heart, which weave themselves into the rugged recesses of man's masculine temperament and constitute him a fit member of society, render them entitled to the warmest affections of your heart, and to the generous protection of your arm.

In another part sits a sister clad in deep mourning, with a number of little children about her. The solemnity which sits upon the countenance, and the sad melancholy which lingers in her eyes, declare that her mourning is not all on the outside. She looks upon the little ones and beholds in them the generous and manly features of their sire, but his place his vacant: And pray, where is he? Oh! as the sturdy oak of the forest is laid low by the shaft from heaven, so has their dear father fallen by an arrow from the bow of a strong archer, and these young and tender branches which have sprung forth from his roots, only are left to perpetuate his name. None but God knows the anguish of that sister's heart, as she hides her face, and pours forth her grief in flowing streams of tearful eloquence. But stay, my hand, open not those wounds afresh when thou hast no balm to bind them up: but may the Lord, whose province it is to comfort all that mourn, and to bind up the broken-hearted, soothe the sorrows of those afflicted ones, and pour the oil of consolation into their grieved and wounded spirit.

When, oh! when shall human grief and woe come to a final end? Thank kind heaven, there is a time when these must cease. In the times of the restitution of all things, when the son of the virgin shall have disarmed death of his power and triumphed over every foe of man; then shall the tree of life spread wide its branches, bloom in eternal spring, and exhale his rich and life-giving odours to the breeze, carrying life, health, and joy upon its balmy wing to every department of God's creation. "Behold we bring you glad tidings of great joy which shall be unto all people."

I have not performed this long journey without encountering *some few* hardships, but I will not mention them; suffice it to say, that I am well at present. The past is over and gone, and I leave the future with my master. You certainly have an interest in my prayers day and night, and I hope you will send up a good wish occasionally for me; yes, even for me. I need it. My heart is full, and I can write no more upon these matters.

Let me now tell you something about a thunderstorm at sea. I have crossed the Atlantic three times—once the German and Black seas, and all about the Levante, besides sailing much on the American waters; but never, no, never before did I witness nature in such a rage on the deep, as once on this last voyage off the island of Candia, about the 7th of December. The sun sat behind the rising bulwarks of a dark and gloomy cloud as though he would not look upon the scene that awaited us: this said to the experienced tar, "there is danger on the deep." About six o'clock in the evening, the breath of the monster reached us: all hands aloft furling sails. The sky became suddenly black—the sea began to roll in upon our weather-beam and lash the hull of our ship, tossing her from surge to surge with as much ease as a giant would sport with an infant. The scene became grand. Our vessel stood on her course—wind on her larboard quarter, and under fore and close-reefed maintopsail only; while thunders loud and long uttered their voices from on high, and rolled through the vaulted canopy as if clothed with the official mandate from Jehovah for the sea to give up its dead. The lightnings issued from the womb of darkness in fiery streams of blazing vengeance to light up the terror of the storm. A feeling of solemnity and awe rolled across my bosom as I gazed upon the troubled deep, raging in the wildness and fury of a tempest. The spray of the clipped surge was frequently whirled on the wing of the eddying currents like mighty cascades upon our deck, while the rain descended like torrents from the mountains. Abroad on the deep, the crested billows rolled high their fleecy heads, and threw up thin sheets of foam in great majesty, coruscating in the lightning's glare; and for a few minutes it really appeared to me that the elements had engaged in a pitched battle—the crown of sovereignty to be awarded to the victor. The winds howled through our almost naked shrouds like a thousand winged spirits waiting to chaunt our requiem; but under the providential care of HIM who governs the winds and the waves, and who formed the ocean from his palm, our gallant barque bore us safely out the gale. Then said I—

> "God speed thee, good ship, on thy pathway of foam,
> The sea is thy country, the billow thy home."

When the light of the next morning had dawned upon us, I arose and went out upon deck, and found our lady of the deep attired in full dress, bearing us over the bosom of the gently rolling billow, apparently as careless and unconcerned as though nothing had happened; and, safely has she brought us into port, so I will sing—

> Now on Europe's shores we're landed,
>   Far away from ocean's roar;
> Where howling winds and rolling surges,
>   Disturb our anxious hearts no more.
>
> Still is every note of tempest,
>   Calmly sleeps the peerless wave;
> An emblem of our friends departed,
>   Whose dust reposes in the grave.
>
> Thanks to Him who holds the billow,
>   And rides aloft on fleecy clouds;
> Let heaven, earth, and seas adore him,
>   With all the vast unnumber'd crowds.
>
> Worthy! worthy is the Saviour!
>   Who, for sinners, once was slain;
> Swell! oh, swell! the joyful anthem,
>   All ye wretched sons of men.
>
> Come unto this bleeding fountain,
>   Meek and lowly you must be;
> Bear the cross and wash in Jordan,
>   Then from guilt he'll set you free.

My poetic organ is not largely developed, so for the correctness of the measure and rhyme of these few lines I will not be responsible.

When in Bavaria I wrote brother Joseph a long letter; it was sometime in August last. I hope he received it, for I think it would do him good—at least it was written with that intention; and I sent one to my wife at about the same time: the answers I hope to receive when I get to Bavaria again.

Fare you well; I love you all, I pray for you all, and by the grace of God, I always shall. I am your brother, far away, and yet near,

ORSON HYDE.

Regenshurgh, January 30, 1842.

TO BROTHER PRATT ALONE,

Sir,—I have thought proper to send this letter to you also, for the same reasons as are assigned in the other. You will therefore publish them both together, if you shall think proper to do any thing with them. The whole was written in Trieste, except these last lines. Not having a convenient opportunity to send them from that place, I brought them with me here to Regensburgh. I now have the pleasure of acknowledging the receipt of your two letters, and one from my wife and brother Joseph, dated 14th November last. I was thrice glad to hear from you all: I laughed and cried altogether. I have no room here to reply, but you may hear from me again by and by.

Dear Brother,—I have not forgotten looking at you through the crevices of a prison, neither have I forgotten what my thoughts were at that time; but if I had had the strength of a Sampson, then was the time that I would have used it for your deliverance. I need not be particular to explain my own situation at that time; "but God be thanked that I am where I am." If enemies are strong and many, nail your flag to the spanker gaff, keep close to the wind, and if your metal is not heavy enough, the artillery of heaven will play upon them.

ORSON HYDE.

LETTER III.[A]

[Footnote A: This letter and the following are of much earlier date than the two preceding, and have either wholly or in part appeared previously in the *Millennial Star*.]

Alexandria, Nov. 22, 1841.

DEAR BROTHER PRATT,

A few minutes now offer for me to write, and I improve them in writing to you.

I have only time to say that I have seen Jerusalem precisely according to the vision which I had. I saw no one with me in the vision; and although Elder Page was appointed to accompany me there, yet I found myself there alone.

The Lord knows that I have had a hard time, and suffered much, but I have great reason to thank him that I enjoy good health at present, and have a prospect before me of soon going to a civilized country, where I shall see no more turbans or camels. The heat is most oppressive, and has been all through Syria.

I have not time to tell you how many days I have been at sea, without food, or how many snails I have eaten; but if I had had plenty of them, I should have done very well. All this is contained in a former letter to you, written from Jaffa.

I have been at Cairo, on the Nile, because I could not get a passage direct. Syria is in a dreadful state—a war of extermination is going on between the Drewzes and Catholics. At the time I was at Beyrout, a battle was fought in the mountains of Lebanon, near that place, and about 800 killed. Robberies, thefts, and murders, are daily being committed. It is no uncommon thing to find persons in the street without heads. An English officer in going from St. Jean d'Acre to Beyrout, found ten persons murdered in the street, and was himself taken prisoner, but was rescued by the timely interference of the Pacha. The particulars of all these things are contained in a former letter.

An American traveller, named Gager, a licensed minister of the Congregational or Presbyterian Church, left Jerusalem in company with me. He was very unwell with the jaundice when we left, and at Damietta we had to perform six days' quarantine before we ascended the Nile. On our passage up he was taken very ill with a fever, and became helpless. I waited and tended upon him as well as our circumstances would allow; and when we landed at Bulack, I got four men to take him to the American consul's, in Cairo, on a litter; I also took all his baggage there, and assisted in putting him upon a good bed—employed a good faithful Arabian nurse, and the English doctor. After the physician had examined him, he told me that he was very low with a typhus fever, and that it would be doubtful whether he recovered. Under these circumstances I left him to obtain a passage to this place. After I had gone on board a boat, and was just about pushing off, a letter came from the doctor, stating that poor Mr. Gager died in about two hours after I left him. He told me before we arrived at Cairo, that he was 27 years of age, and his friends lived in Norwich, Connecticut, near New London, I think. There are many particulars concerning his death which would be interesting to his friends, but I have no time to write them now.

On Sunday morning, October 24th, a good while before day, I arose from sleep, and went out of the city as soon as the gates were opened, crossed the brook Cedron, and went upon the Mount of Olives, and there, in solemn silence, with pen, ink, and paper, just as I saw in the vision, offered up the following prayer to him who lives for ever and ever:

"O Thou! who art from everlasting to everlasting, eternally and unchangeably the same, even the God who rules in the heavens above, and controls the destinies of men on the earth, wilt Thou condescend, through thine infinite goodness and royal favour, to listen to the prayer of thy servant which he this day offers up unto thee in the name of thy holy child Jesus, upon this land where the Sun of Righteousness sat in blood, and thine *Anointed One* expired.

"Be pleased, O Lord, to forgive all the follies, weaknesses, vanities, and sins of thy servant, and strengthen him to resist all future temptations. Give him prudence and discernment that he may avoid the evil, and a heart to choose the good; give him fortitude to bear up under trying and adverse circumstances, and grace to endure all things for thy name's sake, until the end shall come, when all the saints shall rest in peace.

"Now, O Lord! thy servant has been obedient to the heavenly vision which thou gavest him in his native land; and under the shadow of thine outstretched arm, he has safely arrived in this place to dedicate and consecrate this land unto Thee, for the gathering together of Judah's scattered remnants, according to the predictions of the holy prophets—for the building up of Jerusalem again after it has been trodden down by the Gentiles so long, and for rearing a temple in honour of thy name. Everlasting thanks be ascribed unto thee, Father! Lord of heaven and earth, that thou hast preserved thy servant from the dangers of the seas, and from the plague and pestilence which have caused the land to mourn. The violence of man has also been restrained, and thy providential care by night and by day has been exercised over thine unworthy servant. Accept, therefore, O Lord, the tribute of a grateful heart for all past favours, and be pleased to continue thy kindness and mercy towards a needy worm of the dust.

"O Thou, who didst covenant with Abraham, thy friend, and who didst renew that covenant with Isaac, and confirm the same with Jacob with an oath, that thou wouldst not only give them this land for an everlasting inheritance, but that thou wouldst also remember their seed for ever. Abraham, Isaac, and Jacob, have long since closed their eyes in death, and made the grave their mansion. Their children are scattered and dispersed abroad among the nations of the Gentiles like sheep that have no shepherd, and are still looking forward for the fulfilment of those promises which thou didst make concerning them; and even this land, which once poured forth nature's richest bounty, and flowed, as it were, with milk and honey, has, to a certain extent, been smitten with barrenness and sterility since it drank from murderous hands the blood of Him who never sinned.

"Grant, therefore, O Lord, in the name of thy well-beloved Son, Jesus Christ, to remove the barrenness and sterility of this land, and let springs of living water break forth to water its thirsty soil. Let the vine and the olive produce in their strength, and the fig tree bloom and flourish. Let the land become abundantly fruitful when possessed by its rightful heirs; let it again flow with plenty to feed the returning prodigals who come home with a spirit of grace and supplication; upon it let the clouds distil virtue and richness, and let the fields smile with plenty. Let the flocks and the herds greatly increase and multiply upon the mountains and the hills; and let thy great kindness conquer and subdue the unbelief of thy people. Do thou take from them their stony heart, and give them a heart of flesh; and may the sun of thy favour dispel the cold mists of darkness which have beclouded their atmosphere. Incline them to gather in upon this land according to thy word. Let them come like clouds and like doves to their windows. Let the large ships of the nations bring them from the distant isles; and let kings become their nursing fathers, and queens with motherly fondness, wipe the tear of sorrow from their eye.

"Thou, O Lord, did once move upon the heart of Cyrus to shew favour unto Jerusalem and her children. Do thou now also be pleased to inspire the hearts of kings and the powers of the earth to look with a friendly eye towards this place, and with a desire to see thy righteous purposes executed in relation thereto. Let them know that it is thy good pleasure to restore the kingdom unto Israel—raise up Jerusalem as its capital, and constitute her people a distinct nation and government, with David thy servant, even a descendant from the loins of ancient David, to be their king.

"Let that nation or that people who shall take an active part in behalf of Abraham's children, and in the raising up of Jerusalem, find favour in thy sight. Let not their enemies prevail against them, neither let pestilence or famine overcome them, but let the glory of Israel overshadow them, and the power of the highest protect them; while that nation or kingdom that will not serve thee in this glorious work must perish, according to thy word—'Yea, those nations shall be utterly wasted.'

"Though thy servant is now far from his home, and from the land bedewed with his earliest tear, yet he remembers, O Lord, his friends who are there, and family, whom for thy sake he has left. Though poverty and privation be our earthly lot, yet ah! do Thou richly endow us with an inheritance where moth and rust do not corrupt, and where thieves do not break through and steal.

"The hands that have fed, clothed, or shown favour unto the family of thy servant in his absence, or that shall hereafter do so, let them not lose their reward, but let a special blessing rest upon them, and in thy kingdom let them have an inheritance when thou shalt come to be glorified in this society.

"Do Thou also look with favour upon all those through whose liberality I have been enabled to come to this island; and in the day when thou shalt reward all people according to their works, let these also not be past by or forgotten, but in time let them be in readiness to enjoy the glory of those mansions which Jesus has gone to prepare. Particularly do thou bless the stranger in Philadelphia, whom I never saw, but who sent me gold, with a request that I should pray for him in Jerusalem. Now, O Lord, let blessings come upon him from an unexpected quarter, and let his basket be filled, and his storehouse abound with plenty, and let not the good things of the earth be his only portion, but let him be found among those to whom it shall be said, 'Thou hast been faithful over a few things, and I will make thee ruler over many.'

"O my father in heaven! I now ask thee in the name of Jesus to remember Zion, with all her stakes, and with all her assemblies. She has been grievously afflicted and smitten; she has mourned; she has wept; her enemies have triumphed, and have said, 'Ah, where is thy God?' Her priests and prophets have groaned in chains and fetters within the gloomy walls of prisons, while many were slain, and now sleep in the arms of death. How long, O Lord, shall iniquity triumph, and sin go unpunished?

"Do Thou arise in the majesty of thy strength, and make bare thine arm in behalf of thy people. Redress their wrongs, and turn their sorrow into joy. Pour the spirit of light and knowledge, grace and wisdom, into the hearts of her prophets, and clothe her priests with salvation. Let light and knowledge march forth through the empire of darkness, and may the honest in heart flow to their standard, and join in the march to go forth to meet the Bridegroom.

"Let a peculiar blessing rest upon the presidency of thy church, for at them are the arrows of the enemy directed. Be thou to them a sun and shield, their strong tower and hiding-place; and in the time of distress or danger be thou near to deliver. Also the quorum of the twelve, do thou be pleased to stand by, for thou knowest the obstacles which we have to encounter, the temptations to which we are exposed, and the privations which we must suffer. Give us, therefore, strength according to our day, and help us to bear a faithful testimony of Jesus and his gospel, and to finish with fidelity and honour the work which thou hast given us to do, and then give us a place in thy glorious kingdom. And let this blessing rest upon every faithful officer and member in thy church. And all the glory and honour will we ascribe unto God and the Lamb for ever and ever. Amen."

On the top of Mount Olives I erected a pile of stones as a witness according to the ancient custom. On what was anciently called Mount Zion, where the temple stood, I erected another, and used the rod according to the prediction upon my head.

I have found many Jews who listened with intense interest. The idea of the Jews being restored to Palestine is gaining ground in Europe almost every day. Jerusalem is strongly fortified with many cannon upon its walls. The wall is ten feet thick on the sides that would be most exposed, and four or five feet where the descent from the wall is almost perpendicular. The number of inhabitants within the walls is about twenty thousand. About seven thousand of this number are Jews, the balance being mostly Turks and Armenians. Many of the Jews who are old go to this place to die, and many are coming from Europe into this Eastern world. The great wheel is unquestionably in motion, and the word of the Almighty has declared that it shall roll.

I have not time to write particulars now, but suffice it to say, that my mission has been quite as prosperous as I could expect.

I am now about to go on board a fine ship for Trieste, and from thence I intend to proceed to Regensburgh, and there publish our faith in the German language. There are those who are ready and willing to assist me.

I send you this letter by Captain Withers, an English gentleman, who goes direct to England on board the Oriental steamer. He has come with me from Jerusalem. If I had money sufficient I should be almost tempted to take passage on board of her to England, but this I cannot do.

On receipt of this, I wish you to write to me immediately, and direct to Regensburgh, on the Danube, Beyern, or Bavaria. If you know anything of my family, tell me.

My best respects to yourself and family, to brothers Adams and Snow, and to all the saints in England.

May grace, mercy, and peace, from God our Father, and from the Lord Jesus Christ, rest upon you all from this time, henceforth, and for ever. Amen.

Your brother in Christ,

ORSON HYDE.

P.S. Mr. Gager died on the 15th instant, at four o'clock in the afternoon.

LETTER IV.

Jaffa, October 20, 1841

DEAR BROTHER PRATT,

Yesterday I arrived in this place from Beyrout, and just as I was about to start from the American consul's in this place to Jerusalem, at a most enormous price, a company of English gentlemen rode in from Jerusalem with many servants all armed, and they were to return immediately to Jerusalem, and I can go for little or nothing comparatively speaking.

I have only time to say a few words; but through the favour of heaven I am well and in good spirits, and expect, in a day or two, to see Jerusalem.

My journey has been long and tedious, and consequently expensive. If I get back to England with money enough to buy my dinner, I shall think myself well off.

The country is in a terrible state. While I was at Beyrout, a terrible battle was fought in Mount Lebanon, about six hours' walk from Beyrout, between the Drewzes and Catholics. It was said that about four hundred were killed on each side. An English officer, returning from St. Jean d'Acre to Beyrout, was taken by the Drewzes, and would have been killed had not the Pacha come to his rescue.

He said that he found ten human bodies in the street on his way without heads. Thefts, murders, and robberies are taking place almost continually. The American missionaries in Beyrout and Mount Lebanon have had notice from the Grand Sultan, through our minister at Constantinople, Commodore Porter, to leave the country, and a prospect that all the missionaries in Syria will have to leave. This is only conjecture, however. But in this, if it do take place, I can see plainly the hand of Providence. The fact is, this land belongs to the Jews; and the present fermentation thereof shows to me that it is fast working back into the hands of its rightful heirs. God will, in due time, drive out the Canaanites, so that no more a Canaanite shall be found in the land, or in the house of the Lord.

I find that almost an universal anxiety prevails respecting the return of the Jews. The waters are troubled because the Angel has descended. My heart leaps for joy at the prospect of seeing that land, and there fulfilling my mission.

When we left Smyrna for Beyrout, we only took in stores for one week, thinking that would surely be sufficient, as the voyage is usually made in four days; but we were nineteen days on the passage. A number of days I eat snails gathered from the rocks, but the greatest difficulty was, I could not get enough of them. I was so weak and exhausted that I could not go on shore after the slight exertion of drawing on my boots. But that is past; I am now strong and well, and have plenty to eat. I now have nothing but land pirates, in the shape of Arabs, to encounter. An Englishman seems like a brother, let his religion be what it may. Yet I am very partial to the fulness of the gospel; for in it I have great joy.

The servants are now waiting for me, and I must gird on my arms and be off. Yet one thing I will notice, which is this: On my passage from Beyrout to this place, the night before last, at one o'clock, as I was meditating on the deck of the vessel, as she was beating down against a sultry schroke wind, a very bright glittering sword appeared in the heavens, about two yards in length, with a beautiful hilt, as plain and complete as any cut you ever saw. And, what is still more remarkable, an arm, with a perfect hand, stretched itself out and took hold on the hilt of the sword. The appearance really made my hair rise, and the flesh, as it were, to crawl on my bones. The Arabs made a wonderful outcry at the sight; O, Allah, Allah, Allah![A] was their exclamation all over the vessel.

[Footnote A: Lord, Lord, Lord!]

I mention this because you know there is a commandment to me which says, "Unto you it shall be given to know the signs of the times, and the sign of the coming of the son of man."

May the Lord bless you all in England and in America. And I pray that he will bless my wife, and my dear little children; God knows that I want to see them—yea, and all the saints.

I have many particulars that I would like to write, but time will not allow at this time. You will hear from me again by the first opportunity, if the Arabs don't kill me. There is no post here; letters are sent by private conveyance, through friends, &c. God bless you and the cause of Zion is my last prayer.

My love to brothers Snow and Adams, and all the brothers and sisters in the communion: pray for me.

Yours, in great haste,

ORSON HYDE.

THE GATHERING OF ISRAEL.

BY MRS. TINSLEY.

(From the Monthly Chronicle for April.)

A sound hath pass'd through the nations, heard
By the heart alone, when its depths are stirr'd;
Mightier than that of storm-lifted seas,
Than the tempest's rush amid forrest trees;
Mightier than sorrow's earth-born cry,
Than the shout of kings to victory;
And still, where its tale hath gone,
  A voice to the breeze is cast,
"On to Jerusalem, brothers, on!
  We have gain'd our home at last!

"Lift up thine head, O Israel! yet
From the depths of the darkness round thee set;
Rejoice, for the chosen of the Lord
Have listened once more to His living word;
Calling them forth from the nations around,
To the hallow'd rest of their father's ground:
And still, as the goal is won,
  Let the thrilling shout be past,
On to Jerusalem, brothers, on!
  We have gain'd our home at last!

"Was the scoffer strong in the days of old,
Fenced by his idols of dust-won gold,
Mocking their hope, while his footsteps trod
With the prophet-gather'd hosts of God?
Heed him not now in the times that be,
For ours is no common destiny;
But, with true armour, won
  From the stores of the mighty past,
On to Jerusalem, boldly on!
  We have gain'd our home at last!

"Did the desert of old yield its gushing wave,
For the pilgrim-fathers their thirst to lave?
Did the vision of God before them stand,
Guiding their steps to the promis'd land?
And shall we, their children, all forget
That this mighty arm is our refuge yet?

No! by the hope whereon
  We have lean'd through the stormy past!
On to Jerusalem, brothers, on!
  We have gain'd our home at last!

"There flow the waters that flow'd of yore,
Washing no trace from the hallow'd shore;
There rise the hills where our fathers bow'd
When the voice of God shook the riven cloud;
And the boughs of the stately cedar thrill
With that holy breath, for it stirs them still:
And we, are we call'd upon
  By a voice to the desert cast?
On to Jerusalem, Israel, on!
  We have gain'd our home at last!"

www.ingramcontent.com/pod-product-compliance
Ingram Content Group UK Ltd.
Pitfield, Milton Keynes, MK11 3LW, UK
UKHW042152281224
453045UK00004B/349